Tendrel: A Meeting of Minds

TENDREL:
A MEETING OF MINDS

---

by Anne Waldman

Trident Press
Boulder, CO

Copyright © 2024 Anne Waldman

Without limiting the rights under copyright, no part of this publication may be reproduced, stored in, or introduced into a retrieval system, or transmitted, in any form or by any means (electronic, mechanical, photocopying, recording, or otherwise) without the prior written permission of both the copyright owner and the publisher of this book.

ISBN: 978-1-951226-19-0

Cover by Diana Lizette Rodriguez

Author photo by Kai Sibley

Notes and Bibliography by Shannon Sky

Published by Trident Press
940 Pearl St.
Boulder, CO 80302

tridentcafe.com/trident-press-titles

Acknowledgments:
 With thanks to Zoe Brezsny, Kath DeGennaro, Jade Lasalles, Diana Lizette Rodriguez.

Contents

Introductory Note **i**

Tendrel: A Meeting of Minds **1**

Addenda **35**

  Ginsberg's India **37**

  Notes for Dharma Gaze Panel **43**

  Revolutionary Letter 2021 for Diane di Prima **47**

  Samuel R. Delany in the Rhizome **51**

  Heft **59**

Photos **69**

Afterword **77**

Introductory Note

Dedicated to the wellbeing and long life of the experiment that is the Jack Kerouac School of Disembodied Poetics, founded and still evolving at Naropa University in Boulder, Colorado for half a century.

This account was presented in the book *Recalling Chögyam Trungpa*, edited by Fabrice Midal and published in 2005. Trungpa has been a brilliant Buddhist teacher for myself, Diane di Prima, Meredith Monk, Allen Ginsberg, Jackson Mac Low (all present at the first Naropa Summer of 1974), as well as many poets and artists over the years and thousands of other "seekers," all craving spiritual gnosis. He has been a generative, controversial, and consistent *kalyanamitra* (spiritual friend) and master teacher on the profound path of Buddhist study and practice. Trungpa was never a saint or a god or a savior. But he was a lifeline to the creativity, psychology, and illuminating wisdom of

Tibetan Buddhism. An extraordinary teacher, artist, poet, and visionary.

There has been some interest in having this text in a singular edition. It's a great delight to be published by a lineage of the Trident Bookstore which was founded the same year as Naropa Institute (now University). As our world turns in precipitous ways with war, pandemic, climate crisis, revocation of human and civil rights—I welcome the auspicious occasion to share a sliver of this history.

It has been a blessing, as well as a challenge, to be a founder with others in like-minded communities of infrastructure poetics projects my whole life. It always seemed to me that poetry was a first spiritual impulse. This edition includes an addenda of resonant poems and other related texts and photographs.

AW/Year of the Wood Dragon, 2024

Stray Dog

Chögyam is merely a stray dog
He wanders around the world,
Ocean or snow-peaked mountain pass.
Chögyam will tread along as a stray dog
Without even thinking of his next meal.
He will seek friendship with birds and jackals
And any wild animals.

—Chögyam Trungpa, Rinpoche[1]

TENDREL: A MEETING OF MINDS

One of the most seminal and perhaps fortuitous occasions in the world of contemporary poetics and the world of Tibetan Buddhist psychology and meditation was the arrival of Chögyam Trungpa to a very particular environment in the United States that included what is referred to historically as the "New American Poetry." His primary contacts were with poets and writers associated with the Beat literary movement—a branch of the New American *tree*—principal among them Allen Ginsberg, Diane di Prima, William Burroughs, Gregory Corso, Philip Whalen, Joanne Kyger, and myself. This unprecedented conjunction fostered the Jack Kerouac School of Disembodied Poetics, a wing of the larger Naropa University (then Institute), founded in 1974 in Boulder, Colorado by Trungpa and his closest students, expanded to include, in addition to poets, a range of American Buddhist scholars, artists, playwrights, dancers, political and cultural activists, filmmakers, translators, psychologists, guests from other cultures and traditions—primarily Zen, Native American, Christian, and Jewish mystic.

Trungpa, a reincarnated tulku meditation teacher or *rinpoche*—literally "precious one"—in the Buddhist and Shambhala traditions, had been writing poetry in his own tradition and language for some time and had composed masterful *sadhanas* (practice liturgies) that came from profound meditative states or mind-transmissions (*terma*). He was a master calligrapher as well, and a catalyst for a prodigious range of projects which evolved into meditation centers, the Maitri programs, retreat sites, seminaries, a body of orally transmitted teachings, and the development of strong *sanghas* or spiritual communities in the U.S. and Nova Scotia.

Trungpa taught what is referred to as "dharma art" on many occasions at Naropa. As poet Reed Bye has written in an essay on these specific teachings:

> Dharma means something like form or "is-ness" and refers to the experience of things as they are, free from projections. Art comes from an Indo-European verb root meaning "to fit together:" Dharma Art then refers to anything perceived and put together from the unbiased openness of original mind. Meditation is the practice of gaining direct familiarity with this openness.[2]

Trungpa was an indefatigable "activity demon" and a beloved spiritual leader until his untimely death in 1987. Allen Ginsberg's playful thumbnail sketch of Trungpa reads:

> a reincarnated lama trained from age 2 in various ancient practices aimed at concentrating attention, focus-

ing perception, minding thought-forms to transparency, profounding awareness, tasting consciousness, annihilating ego, & immolating ego-mind in phenomena: a wizard in control of day-dream, conscious visualization & thought projection, vocal sound vibration, outward application of insight, practice of natural virtues, and a very admiral of oceanic scholarship thereof.[3]

The Kerouac School, co-founded and designed by Ginsberg and myself, with early input from Diane di Prima, has had a singular rich history of its own, preserved in part by a significant literary audio archive and several key anthologies, as well as transcribed and written documents. The audio archive contains readings, lectures, and seminars from a constellation of poets and writers (from 1974 to the present). The overall mission—if one could state such a thing—of these core and guest writers at Naropa has been to restore the poet's ancient scholarly and shamanic role as keeper of the culture, as well as manifest as performer, teacher, and social commentator. The archive is proof of these important trajectories and is, in part, a legacy of the invaluable conjunction of Trungpa with the poets, as well as the viability of the vision of the Kerouac School.

The philosopher and critical theorist Jacques Derrida has mulled over the subject of archive with great attention in his book *Archive Fever*, conjuring the sense of *permanence*, of motive from the psychological sense, of a power move to establish canon, and so on. It is a source of irony that a school based on the Buddhist tenet of *impermanence* should hold dear its legacy, which one could say the world needs so that creative and spiritually-minded people of the future—should any remain—will comprehend that not everyone in this historical timeframe was caught up in a maelstrom of greed, violence, and war psychosis. Trungpa spoke often of the dangers of the "four lords of materialism." There is also the very intriguing subject of the "institutionalization"—for want of a better word—of a poetics program inspired, in part, by Buddhist theory and practice. Trungpa, whose dharma teachings have also been archived for posterity, had hoped to establish a "comprehensive library" in Nova Scotia (a safer zone), which would preserve spiritual traditions that he and others perceived as endangered in such a dark age as we now experience upon us.

Many constitutional civil liberties are threatened in America. Quality of education wanes, corporate media controls information, a narrow Christian fundamentalist theocracy holds sway in the US government, and there seems less tolerance for difference and the creative imagination. Religious conflict—or one might say power struggles masked as religious ideology—are pandemic in our world. The planet itself is threatened by criminal stewardship. Walt Whitman warned in *Democratic Vistas*[4] that unless American materialism was tempered by a spiritual influence, the United States would turn into "the fabled damned of nations." His antidote was "adhesiveness" between citizens and "candor" of "poets and orators to come." Trungpa has commented that Whitman's image of universal transitoriness in the poem "Crossing Brooklyn Ferry" "equals Buddhist sutras in this perception."[5] This is not to shift the tone to one of doom and apocalypse but rather to make the point that key to the farsighted activities of Trungpa was a sense of urgency ("don't tarry, don't tarry" is a refrain from a Buddhist chant) and that the friendship and collegiality with a number of poets in this country was in fact an occasion of *tendrel*—auspicious coincidence that has empowered the life and work of many individuals, not least of which are the numerous students that continue to flock to the Kerouac School and maintain a continuity of adhesiveness.

The meetings of the two worlds—Trungpa's—himself a holder of an ancient wisdom tradition which included classical Sanskrit-based poetics, who had narrowly escaped the communist junta in Tibet—and the New American Poetry's—constituting a lineage which in addition to containing and honoring the larger "canons" of a world literature and prosody (Gilgamesh, Homer, Sappho, Dante, Shakespeare, Rimbaud, Yeats) also proposed radical shifts of attention for literature after the Modernist period.

Modernist poet William Carlos Williams's "no ideas but in things" and attention to the "minute particulars" resonates with Buddhist attention to "ordinary mind." Ezra Pound's useful triad *melopoeia* (sound), *logopoeia* (the dance of the intellect), and *phanopoeia* (the image cast on the mind) resembles the Buddhist triad of body, speech, and mind, while Gertrude Stein's attention to tracking the grammar of her own thinking was akin to Buddhist mindfulness and discriminating awareness wisdom.

Allen Ginsberg writes of Trungpa's drama in his progression as a poet:

> Consider the progression of style, from early poems adapted out of Tibetan formal-classic modes, to the free wheeling Personism [term of poet Frank O'Hara] improvisations...and the Guru mind's wily means of adapting techniques of Imagism, post-surrealist humor, modernist slang, subjective frankness & egoism, hip "fingerpainting," and tenderhearted spontaneities as adornments of tantric statement. We see respect & appreciation given to the "projective field" of modern Western poetry...[6]

Chögyam Trungpa had been schooled in Tibetan poetics, which was part of one's training as a reincarnated Buddhist lama. The term for poetry in Tibetan—*snyan-ngag* (Sanskrit *kavya*)—means "ornamental language." This writing is characterized by the use of rhetorical and phonetic ornament, and may be written in prose or verse. There is little deliberate use of rhyme. In the use of quatrains, the lines are 5-15 syllables. The shorter lines are characteristic of archaic and folk poetry. The Sanskrit models are usually over 7 syllables (often 11). Tropes include various sorts of simile, metaphor, and the use of stylized literary synonyms. The Buddhist yogins created a distinctive family of verse forms collectively known as *mgur*, or yogic song as manifested in *A Hundred Thousand Songs of Milarepa*, which are "devotional songs" written to lineage gurus and deities in the Buddhist tradition. One finds many of these characteristics in Trungpa's Sacred Songs, a section of his book *Timely Rain*:

> The corpse, bloated with the eight worldly concerns,
> Is cut into pieces by the knife of detachment
> And served up as the feast of the great bliss.
> Is not this your doing, O Karma Pakshi?
> Although I live in the slime and muck of the dark age,
> I still aspire to see your face.
> Although I stumble in the thick, black fog of materialism,
> I still aspire to see your face.[7]

Trungpa also invoked the notion of "crazy wisdom" as a quality poets had, a sublime compliment and, at times, a misunderstood one. It echoed what the poet John Keats deemed "negative capability," which was the ability to hold contradictory thoughts in the mind "without any irritable reach after fact or reason." It was more like Surrealism and engaged *ulatbamsi*, or an upside-down quality, in language and behavior, as in lines from Trungpa's poem "Samsara and Nirvana":

> A crow is black
> Because the lotus is white.
> Ants runs fast
> Because the elephant is slow.[8]

A later poem of Trungpa's has a very different form and tone, much more in the American "ordinary mind" vein of Williams:

> Glory be to the rain
> That brought down
> Concentrated pollution
> On the roof of my car
> In the parking lot.[9]

The New American Poetry—coming on the heels of World War II—specifically refers to various communities and associated "schools" of writers who at that time thrived outside the literary mainstream and outside what one might call the controlling literary mafias of New York publishing and literary journalism. These individuals and communities fostered numerous small presses, engaged in major literary correspondences and debates with one another, and benefited (some might disagree because there were also differences and rifts between some of these communities) from the famous Six Gallery reading in San Francisco on October 6, 1955 where Allen Ginsberg launched his poem "Howl." A range of poets from these different *loci* convened on historic occasions (Vancouver 1963 and Berkeley 1965), and a full number were represented in Donald Allen's now-classic defining anthology *The New American Poetry,* published by Grove Press in 1964, a book of major import to young writers of my generation at the time.

The schools thus named were The New York School (in

the work of John Ashbery, Barbara Guest, Kenneth Koch, Frank O'Hara, James Schuyler, Kenward Elmslie), Black Mountain School (in the work of Charles Olson, Robert Creeley, Robert Duncan, Denise Levertov, John Wieners), San Francisco Renaissance (in the work of Robin Blaser, Jack Spicer, Robert Duncan [again], Joanne Kyger), and the Beat literary movement (Allen Ginsberg, Gregory Corso, Peter Orlovsky, Lawrence Ferlinghetti, Michael McClure, Diane di Prima, Gary Snyder, Lew Welch). Over the years, the Jack Kerouac School has hosted and continues to host many of the writers associated with these communities and their inheritors, as well as younger poets beyond the boundaries of gender and genre. In addition to the palpable presence within the audio archive, the work of these authors has been present in the Kerouac School curriculum, and many of their books are in the holdings of the Allen Ginsberg Library at Naropa. Writer/composer John Cage was also an early guest at Naropa, along with Jackson Mac Low, Robert Kelly, Armand Schwerner, and Jerome Rothenberg. Mac Low has a range of Buddhist-inspired poems. Robert Kelly is a Tibetan Buddhist practitioner and has studied the Tibetan language extensively. Jerome Rothenberg, major anthologist as well as poet, has been attentive to oral and spiritual poetries for decades and has done his own translation of texts by Milarepa and Marpa. Trungpa Rinpoche knew poet Robert Bly before arriving in America, founding Naropa University, and having a controversial relationship with W. S. Merwin, who had briefly taken Trungpa as a spiritual teacher in 1975.

The scope and influence of the New American Poetry and its attendant offshoots and cross-fertilizations with other writers of the expansive poetry world is an Indra's net of interrelatedness and is thus difficult to codify. Confluences that took place coast to coast continue to be analyzed and commented upon and are somewhat outside the scope of this piece.

Suffice it to say, however, that some of the writers most associated with the Beat movement were already very cognizant of and extremely well-read in Buddhist philosophy and psychology. Gary Snyder had majored in anthropology as an undergraduate at Reed College and then did graduate work at the University of California, Berkeley, where he studied classical Chinese and pursued his Zen Buddhist practice. He received a scholarship from the first Zen Institute, which led to nearly fifteen years in Japan. He and his (then) wife, poet Joanne Kyger, traveled to India with Allen Ginsberg and Peter Orlovsky, where they met the 14th Dalai Lama. Jack Kerouac befriended Gary Snyder, who provoked in him an interest in Buddhism. Kerouac's novel *The Dharma Bums* adopts a veiled Snyder as its central character and triggered the "rucksack revolution," which set young people off "on the road" with a resolute spirituality more at home with Buddhist and Taoist thought than with any Western philosophy. "Meditation is the art of deliberately staying open so that myriad things can experience themselves," Gary Snyder has written.

Kerouac also authored *Some of the Dharma* (musings

from his extensive readings in Buddhism) and a biography of the Buddha.[10] Philip Whalen discovered the writings of D.T. Suzuki while at Reed College (rooming with Gary Snyder), lived in Kyoto in 1967 and then from 1969 to 1971, where he wrote *Scenes of Life at the Capital*. Once back in the States, he moved into the San Francisco Zen Center in 1972 and was ordained as Unsui, Zen Buddhist monk. In 1975, he served as head monk of the Tassajara Zen Center. In 1991, he was installed as abbott of the Hartford Street Zen Center in San Francisco, where after retirement he lived until his death in 2002. Diane di Prima had encountered the Zen teacher Suzuki Roshi in 1962 and has stated:

> I sat because he sat. To know his mind. It was the first time in my twenty-eight years that I had encountered another human being and felt trust. It blew my tough, sophisticated young artist's mind.[11]

Allen Ginsberg had also turned toward Eastern wisdom through the instigations of Gary Snyder and Jack Kerouac, and while in India had spent time seeking out Hindu and Buddhist teachers and meditating in charnel grounds. Although thoroughly saturated in the sophistications and subtleties of Buddhist thinking by the time he met Trungpa, Allen immediately "took on" Trungpa's dharma teaching for his own writing "mind." He had immense curiosity about the machinations of his own mental discourse—his "hangups"—and was assiduously attentive to the particulars of his prolific creative practice. His meeting with Trungpa led to an immediate version of a "dharma poetics." Allen enthusiastically proclaimed his spiritual insights to the world, and his own writing and teaching after this time permeated with references to his guru.

Allen speaks from an interview in 1976 at Naropa with Paul Portugés:

Ginsberg: The Tibetan monks I've talked to all report that Trungpa's experienced—seems to know all the angles. His teaching of meditation is excellent; acute, practical. From his own experience, he's gone to the center and is able to teach it well. He said some amazing things to me, like I was hung up on where does my breath begin and end. I went through it very early, and he gave me the image of the breath continuing, sort of, from one breath to another like an opening up of a telescope. Beautiful. I mean one breath leading to another, like the unfolding or opening up of a telescope. Very beautiful, precise image; and once I thought of it in those terms, it seemed to resolve a psychological, mental thing I had, or self-consciousness I had in proceeding from one breath to the other.

Portugés: But you've always been concerned with breath, much longer than you've been studying in the Tibetan tradition.

AG: That's true; it was implicit in the long-line poems like "Howl."

PP: Has it changed, the poetics of breath, since you've been practicing shamatha, etc?

AG: No, because poetry, poetic practice, is sort of like an independent carpentry that goes on by itself. I think, probably, the meditation experience just made me more and more aware of the humor of the fact that breath is the basis of poetry and song—it's so important in it as a measure. Song is carried on the vehicle of the breath, words are carried out through the breath, which seems like a nice "poetic justice," (laughs)—that the breath should be so important in meditation as well as in poetics. I think that must be historically the reason for the fact that all meditation teachers are conscious of their spoken breath, as poets are. That's the tradition, the Kagyu tradition, that the teachers should be poets. That's the reason for the Naropa Kerouac School of Disembodied Poetics; originally, Trungpa asked me to take part in the school because he wanted the meditators to be inspired to poetry, because they can't teach unless they're poets—they can't communicate."

Allen taught meditation practice regularly as part of his writing workshops, and he sought a resonance to dharma with the poetry of William Blake. He and Trungpa came up with the slogan "first thought, best thought." Allen "turned" Trungpa on to Jack Kerouac and writes in a piece entitled *To America: Kerouac's Pomes All Sizes*:

My own poetry's always been modeled on Kerouac's

practice of tracing his mind's thoughts and sounds directly on the page. Poetry can be "writing the mind," the venerable Chögyam Trungpa phrased it, corollary to his slogan "first thought, best thought," itself parallel to Kerouac's formulation "mind is shapely, Art is shapely." Reading *Mexico City Blues* to that great Buddhist teacher from the front car seat on a long drive from the Karme Choling Retreat Center (1972 called Tail of The Tiger) [Vermont] to New York, Trungpa laughed all the way... "Anger doesn't like to be reminded of fits...The wheel of the quivering meat conception...The doll-like way she stands/ bowlegged in my dreams waiting to serve me... Don't ignore other parts of the mind..." As we got out of the car he stood on the pavement and said, *It's a perfect exposition of mind.*

The next day, *I kept hearing Kerouac's voice all night, or yours and Anne Waldman's...* He said it'd given him a new idea of American poetry, for his own poetry...[13]

Trungpa's *International Affairs of 1979*, subtitled: *Uneventful but Energy-Consuming*, clearly echoes some of Allen's political concerns with his own particular sense of irony:

Where is the spirit of Communism?
Marx, Engels, Lenin—
If they returned and saw what a mess they made in the universe they would be horrified.
We find nobody practicing true communism.

> The Chinese declaration of religious freedom in Tibet
> is humorous:
> You are free not to practice religion!
> And the Panchen Lama beckons the Dalai Lama.
> Opening the door of Sino-Tibetan tourism fooled the
> sharpest and most professional journalist;
> they lost their critical intelligence.[14]

There was a very particular flavor to these poetic exchanges that took place between Trungpa and the Beat writers. Lively, probing. At a "Poets' Colloquium" held in Boulder in 1975, William Burroughs began the conversation challenging Trungpa's reluctance on the issue of "psychic practices" such as astral projection and telepathy and their relevance to spiritual practice.

Trungpa replies:

> Well, I wouldn't say "reluctant," actually, but the question seems to be that these phenomena we experience are made up in our psychic level, which we can't actually share with somebody. They're not as real as a dollar bill. So that seems to be the problem, always. And, also, there's a tendency to get into a new world, a new dimension that nobody can share, that people in the street can't share, can't experience. And further, how much are we making these things up, or are they actually happening? That's the kind of question. No doubt a lot of experience occurred. They do function on an individual level, but do they in terms of public phenomena? Someone might see a TWA jet flying overhead, which is everybody's common knowledge. These other things

are not actually common knowledge. It may be common knowledge to a certain particular circle. That seems to be the problematic point. Are we going to encourage people to pursue something that is purely in their minds or to pursue something they can actually share? And half the world, or even more than that actually, 99 percent of the world, haven't realized who they are to begin with, so it's quite a burden.[15]

At the same colloquium Burroughs and Trungpa discuss and disagree about the propriety of taking a typewriter on retreat.[16] Later, Burroughs comments on this exchange after he's written *The Retreat Diaries*.

This excerpt of Burroughs is from *The Burroughs File* (1976):

Last summer in Boulder I was talking to Chögyam Trungpa Rinpoche about doing a retreat at his Vermont Center. I asked about taking along a typewriter. He objected that this would defeat the whole purpose of a retreat, like a carpenter takes along his tools—and I see we have a very different purpose in mind. That he could make the carpenter comparison shows where the difference lies: the difference being, with all due respect for the trade of Jesus Christ, that a carpenter can always carpenter, while a writer has to take it when it comes and glimpse once lost may never come again, like Coleridge's "Kubla Khan." Writers don't write, they read and transcribe. They are only allowed to access [...] the books at certain arbitrary times. They have to make the most of these occasions. Furthermore I am more concerned with writing than I am with any sort of enlightenment, which is often an ever-retreating mirage like the fully analyzed or fully liberated person. I use meditation to get material for writing. I am not concerned with some abstract nirvana. It is exactly the visions and fireworks that are useful for me, exactly what all the masters tell us we should pay as little attention to as possible. Telepathy, journeys out of the body—these manifestations, according to Trungpa, are mere distractions. Exactly. Distraction: fun, like hang-gliding or surf-boarding or skin diving. So why not have fun. I sense an underlying dogma here to which I am not willing to submit. The purposes of a Boddhisattva and an artist are different and perhaps not reconcilable. Show me a good Buddhist novelist. When Huxley got Buddhism, he stopped writing novels and wrote Buddhist tracts. Meditation, astral travel, telepathy, are all means to an end for the novelist. I even got copy out of Scientology. It's a question of emphasis. Any writer who does not consider his writing the most important thing he does, who does not consider writing his only salvation. — "I trust him little in the commerce of the soul." As the French say: *pas serieux*.[17]

It was interesting—in hindsight—to gauge the response here, to feel a demarcation in the spiritual path of Burroughs, whose writing had in fact "rescued" him from a life of addiction and despair. Because Burroughs had been responsible for the death of his wife in a tragic accident involving a William Tell-like game, I once brought up—in conversation—the story of Padmasambhava, the powerful magician-avatar who brought Buddhism to Tibet, who had been responsible for many deaths before becoming a highly realized Tantric teacher. There was a sense that persons involved with death, transgression, and tragedy were more apt or ripe for dharma. I remember William taking it all in with fascination. His disposition seemed, finally, more existential, or Sufi perhaps, the sense of predestined fate—"it is written"—weighed on him. He was interested, however, in very specific advanced Buddhist practices—dream yoga, tummo, chandali or heat yoga, practiced in Tibet's cold winters, and any kind of mind travel. William was not about to "sign on" to anything, join a *sangha*, give up a sense of himself as a professional writer—a respectful identity earned under duress. He was an *eminence grise*, *un homme invisible*, a consummate hipster. As with John Cage, Trungpa's attitude was, this is a person with considerable *siddhi*, let them be.

The relationship with Allen was much more complex. Allen had taken Rinpoche as his root guru—his *sawet* lama, his fiery *Vajra* master. Trungpa pointedly wanted to pop Allen's role as self-appointed spokesman for the Beat literary generation. It was his job to do this. And pop, as well, Allen's political and cultural activist manifestation, a formidable—and very famous—world-renowned presence. Allen was a major "culture hero." Trungpa challenged and teased Allen about his "aggression." There had been earlier encounters, one at which Allen shaved off his beard at Trungpa's instigation. Trungpa had been goading him about his identity. Trungpa had also demanded at one point that Allen compose on the spot publicly, at which point Allen burst out singing the poems of William Blake.

Their repartee resembled the classical dialogues between gurus and disciples, with the guru pushing on the student's ego. Here is a brief exchange from the same Poet's Colloquium:

Rinpoche: Why do you write poetry?

Ginsberg: I took a vow when I was fourteen years old that if I were admitted to Columbia University I would work hard on the salvation of mankind.

Rinpoche: Did you think you were going to be famous?

Ginsberg: That was not the original intention.

Rinpoche: But the second one?

Ginsberg: You know, I don't think I'm going to be famous. I'm already famous, so the future isn't necessarily fame.

And later:

Rinpoche: If you criticize the government or if you talk about homosexuality or whatever, it would be a real statement on your part, something you take pride in.

Ginsberg: What takes pride in mirroring what went past?

Rinpoche: Well, that still somehow has the residue of the coming out.

Ginsberg: Well, I'm confused. Do you feel that this coming out is just pure ego with no value, or do you think it's a useful work that we do.

Rinpoche: Please don't panic.

Ginsberg: I'm not panicking, now will you please stop that! I was examining very closely what you were saying. I'm an expert in this area. I know my own moves.

Rinpoche: Well, I'm trying to study the sociological or psychological set-up of poets, and how they are aware of the audience. A lot of people begin to deny this completely but it is not quite true. You would like to make a proclamation. People write me a poem sometimes. They say, "please destroy this after you have seen it." But they didn't really want it to be destroyed.[18]

Trungpa also parodies or spins off Allen's opening line from "Howl" (one of the most famous lines in contemporary poetry) with:

The best minds of my generation are idiots,
They have such idiot compassion.[19]

Diane di Prima, a key presence in the early years and development of the Jack Kerouac School, became closer to Trungpa Rinpoche after the death of her own teacher, Suzuki Roshi, and worked on her *ngon-dro* (preliminary practice involving 100,000 prostrations, mantras, and mandala offerings) under the auspices and guidance of the Vajradhatu mandala. A poem from those early years carries a sense of poignant irony that suffering is the "greatest blessing."

TRAJECTORY

suffering, sd the Lama, is the greatest blessing
because it reminds us
to seek the disciplines, like:
I don't drink coffee 'cause I once
had an ulcer; and of the four
"continents" of humans, this, the South
Continent (planet Earth) he says
is best because it is hardest. So this
1970 must be an excellent time
when even the telephone poles scream in agony
when the streets are fire beneath
all our windows,
when even the Bodhisattvas stop their ears.

as if they could.
as if we could, we sit
zazen, retreat to the woods
fast, pray, remember bardos
unwritten, even in Tibet.

they come again.
they have us by the throat.

we break before the image of the future
now no more blood runs
from the wounded Earth. our hope
lies in the giant squid that Melville saw, that was
acres across, our hope
lies in the insect world, that the rustling
Buddha of locusts, of ants, tarantulas
of scorpions and spiders
teaching crustacean compassion might extend hope
to our species.
(the Hopi say that it's been done before
and plant their last corn before coal mines
destroy the weather table)   a child of mine
waits to be born in this.   Tristesse.   Tristesse.
Dolor. Now is no star seen
as it was seen by our fathers
now is no color on the hills, no brightness
in the bay. Now do sea creatures rot
with oily fur
with oily feathers choke on black sand.
the hungry ghosts like a wind
descend on us.[20]

Joanne Kyger, who had an early affiliation with Zen practice, frequently honors and refers to the teachings of Trungpa in her poetry. She also has a long poem on the life of Naropa, the pandit and former abbot of Nalanda University, who was both a wild yogin and university administrator. Here is an excerpt from her poem on Trungpa's death, "MIWOK MANDARIN BOLINAS BAMBOO":

> Anything that is "created"
> > must sooner or later die.
> > > Enlightenment is PERMANENT
> > because we have not produced it
> > we have merely discovered it."
> —Chögyam Trungpa
> > Died April 4, 1987

> > Many years ago
> I am going into San Francisco over Mt. Tamalpais
> to read at a big Poetry Reading
> given by Chögyam Trungpa in honor of the first visit
> > > of the Karmapa.
> I am very nervous   I wonder if the car
> > will make it
> > I think I may die any moment
> When I get to the place of the reading
> > > it is very gracious
> > there is a bar set up backstage
> The poets are given a little bottle
> > with a hand lettered label
> > > saying "LONG LIFE PILLS FROM
> HIS HOLINESS KARMAPA"
> I am so nervous
> I swallow them down right away and feel better

"Whew!"
I ask Michael McClure, Aren't you going to take yours?
He says, I'm going to "save" mine
Years later (still alive) I think of those pills—
They were little seeds
If I'd done a really wise thing
      I would have planted those seeds
          So there would be a whole bunch of seeds
     And everyone could have some
             whenever they wanted them
So now what have I got? the little bottle
    of this story—
           and its own Empty Space."[21]

And a few lines from her playful "Continuing Adventures in the Life of Naropa":

* So *

he gets fired up and burnt up
he is in great pain

burnt out
nobody's home
doing nothing
*okay *
keep that vivid vivid experience
alive

  *Commitment *

Oh teacher let me give you this bowl of food.
It's delicious,
Shall I get you some more?
Yes. Go ask for some more.

So he does and gets beat up.

No second helpings here.[22]

My own long seminal poem "Makeup On Empty Space," written in the 1980's, was inspired by a talk Trungpa gave on the feminine principle:

I am putting makeup on empty space:
all patinas convening on empty space
rouge blushing on empty space
I am putting makeup on empty space
pasting eyelashes on empty space
painting the eyebrows of empty space
piling creams on empty space
painting the phenomenal world
I am hanging ornaments on empty space
gold clips, lacquer combs, plastic hairpins on empty
 space
I am sticking wire pins into empty space
I pour words over empty space, enthrall the empty
 space
packing, stuffing jamming empty space

spinning necklaces around empty space
Fancy this, imagine this: painting the phenomenal
  world
bangles on wrists
pendants hung on empty space
I am putting my memory into empty space
undressing you
hanging the wrinkled clothes on a nail
hanging the green coat on a nail
dancing in the evening it ended with dancing in the
  evening
I am still thinking about putting makeup on empty
  space
I want to scare you: the hanging night, the drifting
  night,
the moaning night, daughter of troubled sleep I want
  to scare you
I bind as far as cold day goes
I bind the power of 20 husky men
I bind the seductive colorful women, all of them
I bind the massive rock
I bind the hanging night, the drifting night, the
moaning night, daughter of troubled sleep
I am binding my debts, I magnetize the phone bill,
bind the root of my pointed tongue
I cup my hands in water, splash water on empty space
water drunk by empty space
Look what thoughts will do   Look what words will do
from nothing to the face

from nothing to the root of the tongue
from nothing to speaking of empty space
I bind the ash tree
I bind the yew
I bind the willow
I bind uranium
I bind the uneconomical unrenewable energy of
 uranium
dash uranium to empty space
I bind the color red I seduce the color red to empty
 space
I put the sunset in empty space
I take the blue of his eyes and make an offering to
 empty space, renewable blue
I take the green of everything coming to life, it grows
 & climbs into empty space
I put the white of the snow at the foot of empty space
I clasp the yellow of the cat's eyes sitting in the
black space I clasp them to my heart, empty space
I want the brown of this floor to rise up into empty
 space
Take the floor apart to find the brown,
bind it up again under spell of empty space
I want to take this old wall apart I am rich in my mind
 thinking of this, I am thinking of putting makeup on
 empty space
Everything crumbles around empty space
the thin dry weed crumbles, the milkweed is blown
 into empty space

I bind the stars reflected in your eye
from nothing to these typing fingers
from nothing to the legs of the elk
from nothing to the neck of the deer
from nothing to porcelain teeth
from nothing to the fine stand of pine in the forest
I kept it going when I put the water on
when I let the water run
sweeping together in empty space
There is a better way to say empty space
Turn yourself inside out and you might disappear
you have a new definition in empty space
What I like about impermanence is the clash
of my big body with empty space
I am putting the floor back together again
I am rebuilding the wall
I am slapping mortar on bricks
I am fastening the machine together with delicate wire
There is no eternal thread, maybe there is thread of
 pure gold
I am starting to sing inside about empty space
there is some new detail every time
I am taping the picture I love so well on the wall:
moonless black night beyond country-plaid curtains
everything illuminated out of empty space
I hang the black linen dress on my body
the hanging night, the drifting night, the moaning
 night
daughter of troubled sleep

This occurs to me
I hang up a mirror to catch stars, everything occurs to
  me out in the
night in my skull of empty space
I go outside in starry ice
I build up the house again in memory of empty space
This occurs to me about empty space
that it is nevered to be mentioned again
Fancy this
imagine this
painting the phenomenal world
there's talk of dressing the body with strange
  adornments
to remind you of a vow to empty space
there's talk of the discourse in your mind like a
  silkworm
I wish to venture into a not-chiseled place
I pour sand on the ground
Objects and vehicles emerge from the fog
the canyon is dangerous tonight
suddenly there are warning lights
The patrol is helpful in the manner of guiding
there is talk of slowing down
there is talk of a feminine deity
I bind her with a briar
I bind with the tooth of a tiger
I bind with my quartz crystal
I magnetize the worlds
I cover myself with jewels

I drink amrita
there is some new detail every time
there is a spangle on her shoe
there is a stud on her boot
the tires are studded for the difficult climb
I put my hands to my face
I am putting makeup on empty space
I wanted to scare you with the night that scared me
the drifting night, the moaning night
Someone was always intruding to make you forget
  empty space
you put it all on
you paint your nails
you put on scarves
all the time adorning empty space
Whatever-your-name-is I tell you "empty space"
with your fictions with dancing come around to it
with your funny way of singing come around to it
with your smiling come to it
with your enormous retinue & accumulation come
  around to it
with your extras come round to it
with your good fortune, with your lazy fortune come
  round to it
when you look most like a bird, that is the time to
  come around to it
when you are cheating, come to it
when you are in your anguished head
when you are not sensible

when you are insisting on the
praise from many tongues
it begins with the root of the tongue
it begins with the root of the heart
there is a spinal cord of wind
singing & moaning in empty space[23]

My oral poem "Skin Meat Bones," in which the three words become notes that are sung in varying registers resonate with the mantra OM AH HUM. A poem entitled "Pratitya Samutpada" has "tathagata" embedded in its refrain. A trip to Vietnam inspired the long piece "DARK ARCANA/Afterimage or Glow," which is a series of dharmic questions on the nature of war and colonialism. The book-length poem, "*Structure of the World Compared to a Bubble*"[24] takes the stupa at Borobudur in Java as a paradigm for Buddhist exploration, laying out the path of the Boddhisatva in a ritual walking meditation. Many of my writings over the years have attempted to actualize dharma insight and inspiration.

Thus the conversations, readings, performances, collaborations, panel discussions, poems and the like, occurring with many of the poets who passed through the Naropa gates, particularly those I've cited as "Beats" (this is a historical and handy term but does not convey the full complexity of the individual writers or their work), constitute what I perceive to be an as-of-yet unacknowledged body of uniquely articulated and salutary "dharma-poetics"—that derives from Buddhist psychology and philosophy around such issues as spontaneous mind, the is-ness of language, the sense of "right view," of co-emergent wisdom (similar to Keats's "negative capability"), "intentionality," "first thought, best thought," "things are symbols of themselves" (*Mahamudra*). My own personal poetics has evolved with insights through Buddhist study and practice. It is always interesting to observe where the meditator's mind and the poetry mind might resonate and to be able to describe the processes of mind as an artist (which Buddhism does to such discriminating degrees). As a writer, the bottom line was considering the very nature of thinking, of the watcher, and the notion of being willing to give up that "shadow," your twenty-four-hour-a-day commentator who follows you constantly. What does that mean to a writer? Is it the watcher who gathers up sense perceptions and writes them down at the end of the day? What is the ego of your art? Is it necessary? *Dzinba* means fixation or "holding." Do you need fixation to survive? Are you genuine? Are you appropriating? And in what way? Are you writing in a way that's simply in fashion? What is the ultimate goal?

> Well, while I'm here I'll
> do the work—
> and what's the Work?
> To ease the pain of living.
> Everything else, drunken
> dumbshow.
> 			(Allen Ginsberg, "Memory Gardens," 1969)[35]

Are you motivated by greed? And so on. These were basic questions for any sentient being let alone the ambitious artist. Do artists require special pleading? Do you need the discursive mind that always comments on *how you are doing?* Do you need passion, ignorance, and aggression to be an artist? Isn't Burroughs's assertion that the work can't be legitimate unless the art is the only salvation for the artist too extreme? Isn't this, in fact, a time of grieving where as human beings we are being called upon to use Art as *upaya*—skillful means—on the boddhisattva path? Theodor Adorno asserts in his famous statement, "To write poetry after Auschwitz is barbaric." The dharmic answer might be *There already is poetry. There must be. To ease the pain of living. To wake people up.* To create alternative realities—cultural interventions—in the samsaric world of passion, aggression, ignorance. To propagate sanity.

Trungpa clearly stated from the beginning of the visionary Naropa project that he hoped poets could make the Buddhists more articulate through original speech and mind and that the poets might benefit by sitting meditation, which would provide a greater grounding to their lives and benefit others. And that there be no conflict between poetry and religion. Allen and I declared in our "mission statement" in 1974:

> Though not all the poetry teachers are Buddhist, nor is it required of the teachers and students in this secular school to follow any specific meditative path, it is the happy accident of this century's poetic history—especially since Gertrude Stein—that the quality of mind

and mindfulness is probed by Buddhist practice. There being no party line but mindfulness of thought and language itself, no conflict need arise between religion and poetry, and the marriage of two disciplines at Naropa is expected to flourish during the next hundred years.

Allen Ginsberg also wrote in 1978:

Whatever the fate of The Jack Kerouac School of Disembodied Poetics, some climactic event has taken place in American poetry which will leave its imprint of frankness and wisdom on future American lyric thought.[26]

Addenda

GINSBERG'S INDIA

As a little digression here, which is relevant as it relates to my sense of poetic lineage and has to do with the travels of certain Beat literary writers and my long association with Allen Ginsberg. It was inspiring to me that Allen and other poets associated with the Beat literary movement had aspirations and interest and had already studied the arts and poetry and the languages (Sankrit, Hindi) and the religions of India (primarily Hinduism and Buddhism).

Allen's India was a constant source for his poems even as he struggled with notions of time, prophecy, and the notion of the *arka* in the preserver deities and his notion of Hare Krishna returning in the Age of Pain, our world, time of Kali Yuga. He had his own sense of an American vortex, which needed the form of "sutra."

> I call all powers of imagination
> To my side in this auto to make prophecy
> All Lords
> Of human kingdoms to come
> Shambu Bharti Baba naked covered with ash

Kaki Baba fat-bellied mad with the dogs
Dehorahava Baba who moans Oh how wounded, how wounded
Sitaram Onkar Das Thakur who commands
Give up your desire

Satyananda who raises two thumbs in tranquility
Kali Pada Guha Roy whose yoga drops before the void
Shivananda who touches the breast and says OM Sri-mata
Krishnaji of Brindaban who says take for your guru
William Blake the invisible father of English visions
Sri Ramakrishna master of ecstasy eyes
Half closed who only cries for his mother
Chaitanya arms upraised singing & dancing his own praise
Merciful Changa judging our bodies
Durga-ma covered with blood
Destroyer of battlefield illusions
Million-faced Tathagata gone past suffering
Preserver Harekrishna returning in the age of pain ....
   Come into my lone presence this vortex named Kansas.

(from "Witchita Vortex Sutra" 1966)[27]

The key notion (I touched on earlier) is "vortex" here, that the vortex is the point of maximum energy, generative energy—and all experience rushes into this vortex, all the past that is vital, all the past that is capable of living into the future. Here, you have the vortex of Kansas welcoming a Hindu pantheon of gurus and deities still on Allen's mind after four years.

Ginsberg met the past in India in terms of a continuum of a deep and complex spiritual tradition that was aloud in its "soundings" of mantra and ritual observance and practice with its many syncretic and tantric layers—shamanic, Hindu, Buddhist, Sufi, Bon, and the mind-altering drugs, entheogens—in particular, the ganja that set the mind in a continuous, reflective present that reverberated with insight into the bodily condition and mind's liberation of body up against the notion of bhatki (devotion), egolessness, and the very real problems of poverty, overpopulation, government negligence, the promises of a more compassionate Marxist-Socialist version of society, and so on. And Allen met the vortex in the street—as I did, ten years later—which still exists in so many parts of India, endless and ageless.

So you had India, which was this syncretic vortex itself. It was an amazing "fit" with the restless psyche of Allen Ginsberg that had reverberations into his own writing. His meeting with the poets of Calcutta—especially Sunil Ganguly, a deep and lasting friendship there—and poets of other parts of India was so important. Some of these poets later traveled to the States in the 80s under the Committee on Poetry, with which I was also involved. I traveled to India, then, as Allen's representative, to meet with some of the poets who would later be invited to the US to read at various universities.

The poetic tradition in Calcutta continues to be ongoing and rich. The Kolkata Book Fair, which I have visited in recent years, along with several trips to Calcutta, primarily to the bookshops along College Street that I also visited during my first trip to India in 1973, has been going since 1976.

In any case, it's an interesting web. One can be of a different generation from one's consociates, be on the similar vectors, and one might come to the same place from different perspectives yet share the experience in many different ways. Clifford Geertz uses this metaphor to discuss, among other things, the cosmology of Hindu Bali. Everything has its own timeframe, lives and dies in a day, or seventy years, but many timeframes intersect in vital synaptical ways. The India story for poets is like that. It's the consociational vortex.

Eliot Weinberger commented during the symposium on the Beats at the Asia Society that these Beat exploratory adventures in India were the last adventures in American poetry.[28] I consider myself part of that adventure, in the swath of it. And this interests me in terms of how contemporary poets find their own stance, their own ethos looking into the darkness of their own time, those generative "off cells" seeking sources for gnosis and poetry. But it also saddens me as I think of the insularity of certain literary old boys clubs that are still beholden to a certain yoke of tradition. Or experimental tradition that blurs identity and privilege into a kind of experimental ethos cut off from its roots.

A notion of ritualized performance comes to mind. Of an intervention.

That's why it was refreshing to first see Allen lighting incense on stage, with some dharmic images, chanting and playing the harmonium.

One started to associate Allen's political activity with mantra. And, I think, this is perhaps the most interesting exchange and what stands out so much about Ginsberg's India intervention on the North American continent. That mantra was brought into public political activist space and protest in this way.

It's the rhizome—the underground horizontal tuber system, an Indra's net of conjuncts, associations, possibilities, awakenings. And there are traces and overlappings, and the notion of tendrel—auspicious coincidences—everywhere in this fascinating lore and history.

from Asia Society
Symposium on the Beats,
NYC, 2008

NOTES FOR DHARMA GAZE PANEL

How we can go deeper into our writing and consciousness? is the question here.

The dharma gaze, the spiritual gaze, the meditative practitioner's gaze is a subject for scrutiny. And how that informs our lives, our view, our discipline, our empathy, our practice—our creative work, our writing, our thinking, our daily rituals.

What are our creation myths? Where are we drawn to?

Is it inherited? Are we born inside a worldview, a creation myth, a cosmology, a cosmogony?

What is our worldview, inherited or chosen, where is our poetry? Meditation? Tonglen? What is our practice and what is this?

What strengthens our work, our resolve, our life?

There is no human dimension in any period of history without poetry, some have noted this.

& poetry is the first religion according to Novalis.

That was my understanding, but I yearned for a description of what I already had inkling of—the sacredness of life in language.

What drew me to poetry was its embodying a recognition of the sacredness of life. What drew me to Buddhism was its connection to poetry, and to Tantric Buddhism was the high energy construct of the practice—the wild mind, the crazy wisdom, its connection to shamanism, to animism, tantric Hinduism—that the myriad iconography is a representation of your own mind on which you must work and rely—tame it so it can be even more powerful in the world. Poetry was my *upaya*, my skillful means.

Wanting to bow, wanting to prostrate to an awakened consciousness.

I've spoken about Documentary Poetics being one way to confront the demons & dystopia of the Anthropocene, Docu Po as a practice within our creative work.

I participated this past weekend in a conference on Rocky Flats in conjunction with a very powerful exhibit around the history and the deadly practices of nuclear dystopia at the Arvada Museum in conjuction with the Rocky Flats Cold War Museum.

From that particular place just down the road here—creating plutonium pits for warheads, 70,000 of them, each warhead with the ability to wipe out our entire so-called civilization. It brought vividly back the work we were doing in the seventies & eighties & nineties and continue in this new century around nuclear weaponry and waste, because plutonium has a half-life of nearly a quarter of a million years.

& it also made me grateful for a non-theistic dharmic view that recognizes suffering and impermanence and activist compassion, and a view that we need to wake up, that there is no external salvation here below, and we must be grateful for what is called sangha in Buddhism. A *sangha* is a spiritual community, people on a path together.

Working with the triad of ground path fruition. Working with mind. With empty space. With "thinking," with coming back to the breath and with what is called a bodhisattva vow to help the consciousness and stability of others. Do no harm. Cease fire. Peace now.

The Jack Kerouac School of Disembodied Poetics
Summer Writing Program, 2016
ongoing pedagogy

REVOLUTIONARY LETTER 2020
FOR DIANE DI PRIMA

"to preserve the element of unknown places"
                                            -Aldo Leopold

I.

Dear Regenerative Agriculture,

Come our way

All the extra carbon could be taken care of....

In a De-Growth Utopia

Concern that we are just "procedural"?

Know your soil.

2.

Just so you know:
Diane di Prima had full body-spirit of outrage
She was transmitting grounded-ness
Although she studied angelicity
& systems of dialectic art
She was a shield & she was sanctuary

She knew the skandas
Never a hall of mirrors
She opened the field
Justice for all – an ecology of practice & mind

3.

Know sunset, sunrise
Crimson hues of dawn
Moonset, moonrise
How you waited
Know their tongues
What they speak to you
What the thunder said:

Do you want blood to
come out of me?

Chaos of storm, of fire

Learn lessons of sorrow
Tithe time

Come with your punctuation
Your dharma vow

Be ready to evacuate
Enough for 10 days survival
Keep simple
Have a place to stay
Read The Invisible Committee
Achille Mnembe
The Zapatista Reader
Full Body Burden
The Akashic Records
Sunken Suns

4.

Who stands in the sun
who was meant
for these firestorms?
"Loba"

Ask this every day

Create a shrine of intention
As she did every day.

Jack Kerouac School of Disembodied Poetics,
October 25, 2020

SAMUEL R. DELANY IN THE RHIZOME

"Science fiction isn't just thinking about the world out there. It's also thinking about how that world might be — a particularly important exercise for those who are oppressed, because if they're going to change the world we live in, they - and all of us - have to be able to think about a world that works differently."

-Samuel R. Delany

    and that

    the reticulated
    would be kind embryology

    held for students

    & students would be ubiquitous for they would be aloft

    for him
    in him as lexicon
    he said "eschew the first-person I"

he betters all essential students
& they don't fray
not withstanding o craft the unbearable
o craft, will the world get better?

curious and listen, the voices
inside the character what do they want

violence surrounds, and endarkening & he stays

steady he does and o he stays all the more energetically
plays the ear, complex he says, listen
& your sentence? again?

"we have these peculiar weathers"
at the table, students, a cult circle and
feed on not tainted who hibernate in

devices he suggests provoke
& the student will be off on tangent sentence

dear life?

& man in his narrative will reveal
his fear or never do this
and alight like redemption

there is a stairwell
there is a dark theatre
there is outer space

for it his ethos, student, is liberation
can't say enough stay enough play enough its
taut library inside liberation

spectators of revolutions know
then precipitate participation
& who watched was transformed

in the magical city

was among those

was there another digression come back
in or out landscape perfect logic of it
student another dimension may you know student

come inside this revolution
enchanted by beauty, sez Genet

the white of the paper artifice
of that writing
"may all possess more reality than the signs that mar
  them"

strike the page will not hurt but when ear strikes
I will visit other room and worlds

deposit a trace in my body with your homesick blues
student strike it now or you die

no considered option here in this opinion of "takes"
"drafts"

but daylight provenance
when do you write and where? maybe why

previous page a posthumous sentence
or dimensions converge
much city too and could say "Mu", a city
on "Irreparable" (a planet as we said of Robin Blaser)

& of memory, a twist
fantasy & *'istorin* get spoken
crucially, "find out for yourself"

get up the crux of our story
web it
better put the talons on

as if in a basement house straight up
into the quantum sphere

where queer might go

draft an impossibility of dialogue encounter
intervention versus interrogation

staying point

not no impossibility, student

student the lore of it and student
had written once New York City

trauma, desire, desire inaugurate the page

& do that for student & others in their cities

you will be springboard
but if you never read books you will be nowhere
you will have to stay writing a tour life
as I, Chip, tell you this

no no don't want *that*

and not reduce passion

would travel in such a way it never happenstance
any reduction to the cut-up
impulse to give the character his way

hidden secret pleasure
connected did it with student complexity

gives giving give most powerful un- psychic pain
intimacy include the mind inflicts would be the velvet

you would not be an "I" he said, never working, that
you tell students
that would not be a prose as purpose

convenient with resistance?

dreamed the orchid

will be my dhalgren

directions encapsulated

repeat this working through mind-whack
for students would marvel
at memory a history at memory's pace where you lose "self"

would walk

he is walking by

that is the rhythm and a cane

spunk and higher voices raise higher

spirit that is unsettled world

in a world student would write upon

could better be watch what I do

follow me but yourself this path reassuring

vertiginous

body is a work

border a tie of sympathy

how, they ask your thousands of pages?

most human teacher "on a roll"

holding

never broken that we know nothing
patience with us, your students

but delight with you

& in lovely duo-figurement is the dreamer

eros a medley
may he be that ever in us
eros a medley

outsider no words were his but his & his sci-fi spiders

no utterance emits where he speaks but his

spectacle he leaves glowing speaking, writing

that text off page from the stage soaring reading

and expressed, that you know bottom nature

this person in *that* story in the valley, o Chip!

most precious belong the myriad directions!

> *The Jack Kerouac School of Disembodied Poetics*
> *Summer Writing Program 2013,*
> *celebrating longtime summer faculty "Chip" Delany*

HEFT

―――――――――

the fable

of the little girl who liked sunlight, so she pulled down the blinds, to keep it all in for herself.

Photo by Anne Waldman. February 2007, Elephanta Island, Mumbai

1.

See it for yourself she said let's go back to the moveable

where did you exist if not before printing type

chromolithography?

laser? thermal? inkjet? digital?

The planet turns

o yes, we were in the tangible-imagination-position

making sounds into letters, imitating birds

letters into prayers

prayers that would not save us

moving the type around

hoping for a color an eye loves

adhesive in 1377

bones, shells, bamboo slips

inscription on the tortoise that says

"see the oracle in your double moon"

or "we will be saved if we carry light"

"why some ages more virtuous, others more evil?"

"why do these questions come to us now?"

    mirrors for thoughts

    rule our wits?

    observe curfew scripts

    curtain up

    old passion dislodged

    mirrors for printers

    o rest eyes upon

    boxes within boxes

    a little heart

    fairy worlds

    shelter, a shaggy hut

    fire up smallest increments

    a swarm of reverie

patience is the game

stand you here

in ink

roll the wheels

a labor of scrolls and temple dwellers

in the wee hours of the phosphorescent star

with phoenix and turtle on a prowl

a whole cosmos moving

toward completion

write the story

can your image be adduced

do we have an audience?

who comes to these ruins

of chisel and memory

what do you have to carry

to arrive

a
sites of ritualized action
a kinesthesia

to survive

as if in trance

hypnotic swerve

what is the dram of

a finite universe?

our time frame nearly up

lift

of landscape

heft of ambivalence

lilt of sublimity

can difficulty be mild?

esoteric, veiled, arcane

a seer of ornaments

will strife save you

a boudoir with lace curtains?

garden of textures

compulsive

end-time scenarios

ecology knows no boundaries

(ideas and acts are foreign bodies, facing themselves
upon the mad patient)

2.

The little girl is a phenomena, a quality magnified, she sings, she resists.
She doesn't worry about reaching a goal. Is there a tomorrow? She would not care.
Her heft is her innocence. Survival is how she plucks herself off the grid.
Her handiwork is lack of guile, lack of suppression. She is a natural mirror of mind.

3.

Ecology knows no boundary. We say border line we say border town. We say duties of our

   darkness.

We see a snake, we run. We confront the smaller deities. We compare dynamics. India. Tibet.

Mecca. Death of dolphin. Detroit of possibilities. Bury more plutonium.

   mountains glazed in rain.

A crucible. Our small hometown. The city. The exile. The charnel ground. We labor the broken

spine and then imprint upon it. We print the symbol for "stand by your word". We

conjure '"mixing it up". We play with phonetics. We work all night. We write small treatises,

we write large epics. We are slogans of ourselves. Polished jade. Jasper. Malachite. Mineral

loves its taste. Ink is the last chance. Documentary should provide mirth. Laughter is a weight.

Documentary is our new hope. We will swell the ranks.

Archive is our desire for future enlightenment. The populace will resound in its

own erotic way to marvel the texture and the dream. The medicine will not save us but be a kind

of mantra you might dance with.

heave/handle thieve/theft tsa tsa ma ma ma weave/weft

"to haven other 'haeftes' in hand" : to test the weight of something by lifting it up

The dance of death resembles the medieval "complaint" which chronicles a sequence of ways

we feel a world falling to pieces. One of many.

The poet stratifies the poem. It's a legacy, it is moral, philosophical

Perhaps it is cosmogonic and suggests the cosmos and is ordered through the stages of creation

Let me be a ritual, the poet says. Let me build a new architecture of light, shade, feather, wind, ink, bone. Lift your head.

Written for the Harry Smith Kavayantra Printshop,
Jack Kerouac School, Naropa
2016

Photographs

L to R: Peter Warshall, Michael Brownstein, Joanne Kyger, Anne Waldman, Allen Ginsberg, Rick Fields, Ed Sanders. Photo by Rachel Homer. 1970s, Naropa University parking lot.

L to R: Anne Waldman, Allen Ginsberg, Diane di Prima. Glenn Miller Auditorium, University of Colorado, summer 1974, Boulder.

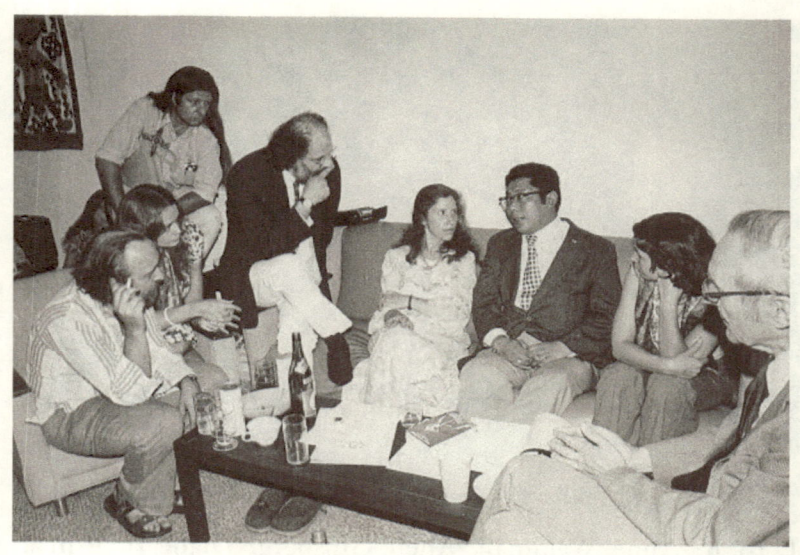

L to R: Jerome Rothenberg, Anne Waldman, Peter Orlovsky, Allen Ginsberg, Diane di Prima, Chögyam Trungpa Rinpoche, Barbara Dilley, William S. Burroughs. Circa 1974-1975, Boulder.

Anne Waldman with Chögyam Trungpa Rinpoche. Photo by Allen Ginsberg, courtesy of Fahey Klein Gallery Los Angeles. July 1978, Boulder.

Anne Waldman reads at Naropa Institute on Pearl Street.
Photo by Christopher Felver. 1983, Boulder.

L to R: Gary Snyder, Allen Ginsberg, Ed Sanders, Anne Waldman. Naropa Summer Writing Program. Late 1980s, Boulder.

Naropa Summer Writing and Poetics tent. 1994, Boulder.

AFTERWORD

Holy Dissonance

What is a fantasy of catastrophe like? It keeps you wakeful and curious. The disjunct here, a cognitive dissonance for someone so young.

"Often I am permitted to return to a meadow.

as if it were a scene made up by the mind

that is not mine but is a made place

that is mine"

> (Robert Duncan, from *The Opening of the Field*)

What dharma (truth) or myth is structuring my imagination?

NOTES

1. Trungpa, Chögyam. *The Collected Works Of Chögyam Trungpa Volume Seven*, edited by Carolyn Rose Gimian. Shambhala Publications, 2004.
2. Bye, Reed. "No One Spoke: Chögyam Trungpa's Teachings on Dharma Art." in *Civil Disobediences*, edited by Anne Waldman and Lisa Birman. Coffee House Press, 2004, pp. 224-239.
3. Allen Ginsberg in the Naropa Archives.
4. see Whitman, Walt. *Democratic Vistas: The Original Edition in Facsimile*, edited by Ed Folsom. University of Iowa Press, 2010.
5. Ginsberg, Allen. "Whitman's Influence: A Mountain Too Vast to Be Seen" in *Deliberate Prose: Selected Essays, 1952-1995*, edited by Bill Morgan. Perennial, 2001, p. 333.
6. Ginsberg, Allen. "Introduction to First Thought Best Thought" in *Deliberate Prose: Selected Essays, 1952-1995*, edited by Bill Morgan. Perennial, 2001, p. 460.
7. Trungpa, Chögyam. *Timely Rain: Selected Poetry of Chögyam Trungpa*, edited by David I. Rome. Shambhala, 1998, pp. 170-171.
8. ibid., p.46.
9. ibid., p.58.
10. see Kerouac, Jack. *Wake Up: A Life of the Buddha*. Penguin Books, 2009.
11. Waldman, Anne, ed. *The Beat Book: Writings from the Beat Generation*. Shambhala Publications, 1996, p. 122.
12. Ginsberg, Allen. *Spontaneous Mind: Selected Interviews, 1958-1996*, edited by David Carter. Perennial, 2002, p. 399.
13. Ginsberg, Allen. "To America: Kerouac's *Poems All Sizes*" in *Deliberate Prose: Selected Essays, 1952-1995*, edited by Bill Morgan. Perennial, 2001, p. 374.

14. Trungpa, Chögyam. *Timely Rain: Selected Poetry of Chögyam Trungpa*, edited by David I. Rome. Shambhala, 1998, pp. 96-99.
15. Trungpa, Chögyam, et al. "Poets' Colloquium." in *LOKA 2: A Journal of Naropa Institute*, edited by Rick Fields. Anchor/Doubleday, 1976, p. 164.
16. ibid., 169-171.
17. Burroughs, William S. *The Burroughs File*. City Lights Books, 1984.
18. Trungpa, Chögyam, et al. "Poets' Colloquium." in *LOKA 2: A Journal of Naropa Institute*, edited by Rick Fields. Anchor/Doubleday, 1976, pp. 167, 172.
19. Trungpa, Chögyam. *Timely Rain: Selected Poetry of Chögyam Trungpa*, edited by David I. Rome. Shambhala, 1998, p. 62.
20. di Prima, Diane. *Selected Poems, 1956-1976*. North Atlantic Books, 1977.
21. Kyger, Joanne. *Just Space: 1979–1989*. Black Sparrow Press, 1991.
22. Kyger, Joanne. *Again: Poems 1989-2000*. La Alameda Press, 2001.
23. Waldman, Anne. *Helping the Dreamer: Selected Poems 1966-1988*. Coffee House Press, 1989.
24. see Waldman, Anne. *Structure of the World Compared to A Bubble*. Penguin Poets, 2004.
25. Ginsberg, Allen. *The Fall of America: Poems of These States 1965-1971*. City Lights Books, 1972, p. 135.
26. Allen Ginsberg in the Naropa Archives.
27. Ginsberg, Allen. *Planet News*. City Lights Books, 1968.
28. see Baker, Deborah. *A Blue Hand: The Beats in India*. Penguin Press, 2008.

Selected Bibliography:

Allen, Donald, ed. *The New American Poetry, 1945-1960 With a New Afterword*. University of California Press, 1999.

Burroughs, William S. *The Burroughs File*. City Lights Books, 1984.

di Prima, Diane. *Selected Poems, 1956-1976*. North Atlantic Books, 1977.

Ginsberg, Allen. *Deliberate Prose: Selected Essays, 1952-1995*. Perennial, 2001.

-----. *The Fall of America: Poems of These States 1965-1971*. City Lights Books, 1972.

-----. *Planet News*. City Lights Books, 1968.

-----. *Spontaneous Mind: Selected Interviews, 1958-1996*. Perennial, 2002.

Kyger, Joanne. *Again: Poems 1989-2000*. La Alameda Press, 2001.

-----. *Just Space: 1979–1989*. Black Sparrow Press, 1991.

Trungpa, Chögyam. *Timely Rain*. Shambhala Publications, 26 May 1998.

Waldman, Anne, ed. *The Beat Book: Writings from the Beat Generation*. Shambhala Publications, 1996.

-----. *Helping the Dreamer: Selected Poems 1966-1988*. Coffee House Press, 1989.

-----. *Vow to Poetry*. Coffee House Press, 2001

Unpublished Addenda by Anne Waldman and Other Texts:

Ginsberg's India
Samuel R. Delany in the Rhizome
Dharma Gaze Panel
Heft

Photo by Kai Sibley

Anne Waldman: Triple Aries, April 2, 1945. Father fought Nazis in WWII in Germany. Mother, Frances LeFevre Sikelianos Waldman, spent a decade in Greece in the Delphi Ideal community of Greek poet Angelo Sikelianos. Was living alone on MacDougal Street, Greenwich Village, NYC, husband at war in Germany. Grew up in New York City's "bohemian" Village. Anne sat on great singer Lead Belly's knee as a baby. She grew up with books of poetry, first poetry reading at Izzy Young's Folklore Center, fell in love with jazz and progressive politics. Blake, Rimbaud, Steve Lacy in her extended family. Started writing seriously as teenager with Beat generation and New York School outside her door. College education of literature, performance, loved Blake, Romantics, psychology studies, but more engaged with reach of world literatures, oral world epics, litany, chant, trance, shamanism, entheogens. Modernists, Gertrude Stein, Mina Loy, Franz Fanon, James Baldwin, open form New American Poetry of Beats and New York School and Black Mountain. Was a decade's-working founder and director of The Poetry Project in 1968 at the historic Dutch Reformed St. Mark's Church in-the-Bowery, home to poets, dancers, artists, filmmakers, painters, activists. Has always championed the bringing of poetry, as well as cultural activism, into public space. Co-founded the Jack Kerouac School of Disembodied Poetics program at Naropa Institute in Boulder, Colorado, on the spine of the North American continent, with Allen Ginsberg and with Diane di Prima in active early years. Waldman continues to work during summers as Artistic Director of the Summer Writing program and guardian of its audio/video literary archive. She was arrested at Rocky Flats with Daniel Ellsberg and Allen Ginsberg in the 1970s, reading poems that challenged deliveries of plutonium for the manufacturing of pits for nuclear warheads. She was part of protests during the Vietnam War, the Chicago Seven trial, and all the doings of counter-cultural intervention in subsequent times—Occupy Wall Street and so on. She works with the Rizoma Collective in Mexico City. Author of over 60 volumes of poetry, poetics, and anthologies including the 1,000-page epic *The Iovis Trilogy: Colors in The Mechanism of Concealment* (Coffee House Press), which won the Pen Center Literary Prize for Poetry. Penguin has published her books over many years, including *Trickster*

Feminism, *Manatee/Humanity*, and *Marriage: A Sentence*. Her album *SCIAMACHY,* which Patti Smith has called "exquisitely potent, a psychic shield for our times," was released in 2020 by Fast Speaking Music in NYC. Recent publications: *"Para ser estrella a medianoche," Become a Midnight Star* (Arrebato Libros, bilingual, Madrid, 2022); anthology *NEW WEATHERS: Poetics from the Naropa Archive* (with Emma Gomis, Nightboat, 2022); and *Bard, Kinetic,* (Coffee House, 2023). Grammy-nominated opera *BLACK LODGE*, with music by composer David T. Little, premiered at Opera Philadelphia Oct 1 & 2, 2022.

OTHER VERY FINE TITLES FROM
TRIDENT PRESS

Blood-Soaked Buddha/Hard Earth Pascal
by Noah Cicero

it gets cold
by hazel avery

Major Diamonds Nights & Knives
by Katie Foster

Cactus
by Nathaniel Kennon Perkins

The Pocket Emma Goldman

Sixty Tattoos I Secretly Gave Myself at Work
by Tanner Ballengee

The Pocket Peter Kropotkin

The Silence is the Noise
by Bart Schaneman

The Pocket Aleister Crowley

Propaganda of the Deed:
The Pocket Alexander Berkman

Los Espíritus
by Josh Hyde

The Soul of Man Under Socialism
by Oscar Wilde

The Pocket Austin Osman Spare

America at Play
by Mathias Svalina

With a Difference
by Francis Daulerio and Nick Gregorio

Western Erotica Ho
by Bram Riddlebarger

Las Vegas Bootlegger
by Noah Cicero

The Green and the Gold
by Bart Schaneman

Selftitled
by Nicole Morning

The Only Living Girl in Chicago
by Mallory Smart

Tourorist
by Tanner Ballengee

Until the Red Swallows It All
by Mason Parker

Dead Mediums
by Dan Leach

Echo Chamber
by Claire Hopple

Launch Me to the Stars, I'm Finished Here
by Nick Gregorio

www.ingramcontent.com/pod-product-compliance
Lightning Source LLC
Chambersburg PA
CBHW020442090526
44586CB00045B/769